Staying Healthy:
Eating Right

Alice B. McGinty

The Rosen Publishing Group's
PowerKids Press™
New York

Published in 1997 by The Rosen Publishing Group, Inc.
29 East 21st Street, New York, NY 10010

First Edition

Book Design: Kim Sonsky

Photo Credits: Cover by Seth Dinnerman

Food Photo Credits: p. 4 © Nancy McFarland/FPG International; pp. 5, 13 by Seth Dinnerman; pp. 6–7, 11, 15–17, 19 © PhotoDisc; pp. 6, 18 © Tom O'Brien/International Stock; pp. 8–9 © Earl Kogler-Corp. Media/International Stock; p. 10 © Frederic Stein/FPG International; p. 14 © Michael Philip Manheim/International Stock; pp. 15, 21 © Artville.

Photo Illustrations: All photo illustrations of children by Seth Dinnerman.

McGinty, Alice B.
        Staying healthy. Eating right. / Alice B. McGinty.
            p.   cm. (The library of healthy living)
        Summary: Discusses the four food groups, the nutrients our body needs, and the importance of healthy eating.
        ISBN 0-8239-5136-7
        1. Nutrition—Juvenile literature. [1. Nutrition.] I. Title. II. Series.
    RA784.M397 1996
    613.2—dc21
                                                                                96-44287
                                                                                    CIP
                                                                                    AC

Manufactured in the United States of America

Contents

Eating Healthy Foods

Have you ever wondered why you're not allowed to eat chocolate cake and jelly beans for breakfast? It's because you need to eat foods that are **nutritious** (new-TRISH-us). Nutritious foods are

4

good for you. They help you grow strong and healthy.

There are many kinds of foods. Oranges, carrots, milk, noodles, and jelly beans are a few. Some foods are nutritious and others are not.

Once you learn which foods are nutritious, you can be a healthy eater!

What Are Nutrients?

Hiding inside most of the foods you eat are **nutrients** (NEW-tree-ents). Nutrients are too small to see. They enter your body when you eat.

There are many different nutrients, and your body needs them all. They help you in many ways.

Some nutrients are body builders. They help you grow big and strong.

6

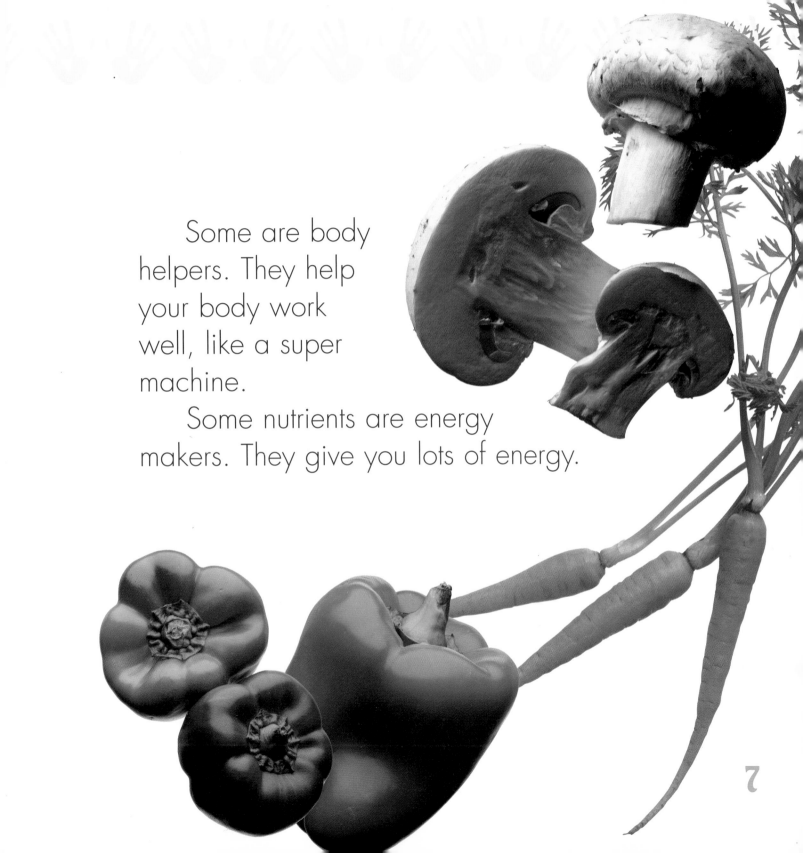

Some are body helpers. They help your body work well, like a super machine.

Some nutrients are energy makers. They give you lots of energy.

7

The Four Food Groups

Nutritious foods are divided into four food groups. The foods in each group have many of the same nutrients. They help your body in many of the same ways.

The four food groups are: grains, fruits and vegetables, milk and dairy, and **proteins** (PRO-teens). To be a healthy eater, you should eat foods from all four food groups every day.

Good nutrition is like a **recipe** (REH-sih-pee). If you follow the recipe, your body will have the nutrients it needs to grow healthy and strong.

The Milk and Dairy Group

Milk, ice cream, and yogurt are foods in the milk and dairy group. They all have a nutrient called **calcium** (KAL-see-um).

Calcium is a **mineral** (MIN-er-ul). Minerals come from the ground. They are soaked up by the roots of plants. When animals, such as cows, eat plants, the minerals enter the cow's milk. When you drink milk, you give your body calcium.

Calcium helps your body build strong bones and teeth. You need a lot of calcium!

Many foods are made with milk, such as cheese, yogurt, butter, and ice cream.

Grains

Bread, cereal, pasta, and rice come from grains that grow as plants. We call these foods **starches** (STAR-chez). They all have important nutrients called **carbohydrates** (car-boh-HY-drayts). Carbohydrates come from energy that the grain plant gets from sunlight. When you eat foods made from grains, the carbohydrates give your body energy.

You use energy all the time, even when you're sleeping. You use energy to breathe, think, and play. It's important to eat many foods from the grain group for lots of energy.

Chances are that your favorite cereals are made of grains, such as oats, wheat, or rice. ▶

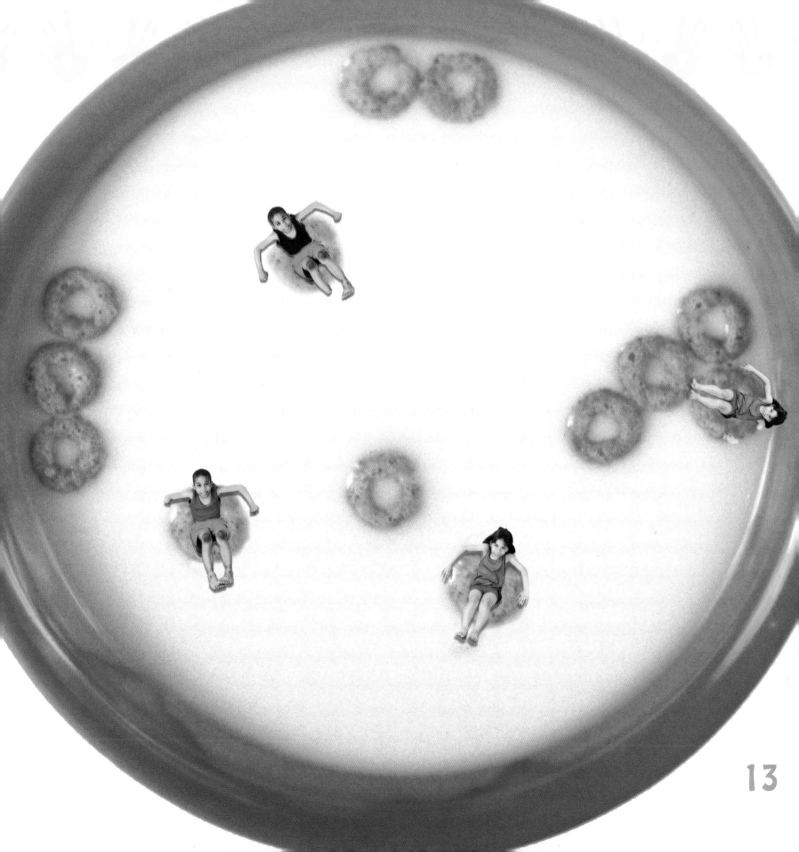

13

Fruits

Fruits have carbohydrates too. These carbohydrates come from the sugar that makes fruit taste sweet.

Fruits that taste sour, such as lemons and grapefruits, are called **citrus** (SIH-trus) fruits. They have a nutrient called **vitamin C** (VY-tah-min SEE). Vitamin C helps make your teeth strong and your gums healthy. It also helps fight germs.

Vegetables

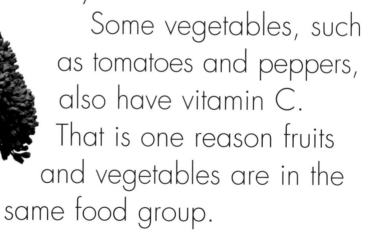

Vegetables have many nutrients. Broccoli has calcium for strong bones and teeth. Spinach has a mineral called **iron** (EYE-ern) that keeps your blood healthy.

Some vegetables, such as tomatoes and peppers, also have vitamin C. That is one reason fruits and vegetables are in the same food group.

Fruits and yellow,
orange,
and
dark
green vegetables have a nutrient that helps your
body make vitamin A. Vitamin A helps your eyes
see well at night and
makes your skin soft
and smooth.

Proteins

What do fish, meats, nuts, beans, and eggs have in common? Together they make up the food group called proteins.

Protein is a nutrient. Proteins are like building blocks. They attach

together to build your body parts. For example, your **muscles** (MUS-ulz), hair, and skin are all built with proteins. As you get bigger, proteins help your body grow.

Peanut butter, baked beans, beef, and chicken all seem very different, but they all have lots of protein.

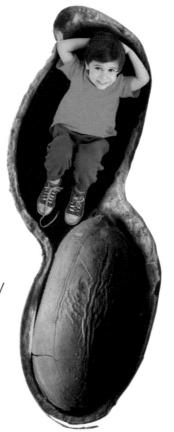

19

Water, Fiber, and Fats

Many nutrients are found in all four food groups.

Water is a nutrient. Your skin, blood, sweat, and other parts of your body are made mostly of water. Fruits, milk, and vegetables have water in them.

Grains, vegetables, and the skins of fruits have **fiber** (FY-ber). Fiber helps your body break down foods to find the nutrients that hide inside.

Fats hide in foods like meat, ice cream, and nuts. Your body needs a little bit of fat to store energy and stay warm. But too much fat isn't good for you.

You need to drink plenty of water every day to stay strong and healthy. ▶

21

Being a Healthy Eater

Soda and candy, such as jelly beans, have few nutrients. They don't help you grow or become strong. Fried foods, like french fries or corn chips, have lots of fat. It is not healthy to eat too many of these kinds of foods.

Be a healthy eater by choosing nutritious foods. Each day you should eat four servings of fruits and vegetables, four servings of grains, three servings of milk and dairy, and two servings of proteins. Follow the recipe for good nutrition for a strong, healthy body.

Glossary

calcium (KAL-see-um) A mineral that helps your body grow strong teeth and bones.

carbohydrate (car-boh-HY-drayt) A nutrient that gives your body energy.

citrus (SIH-trus) A kind of fruit that has a sour taste and contains vitamin C.

fiber (FY-ber) A part of some foods that helps your body break down other foods.

iron (EYE-ern) A mineral that helps your blood stay healthy.

mineral (MIN-er-ul) Something that comes from the ground that is not a plant, animal, or other living thing.

muscle (MUS-ul) A part of the body attached to the bones that allows the bones to move.

nutrient (NEW-tree-ent) Something that a living thing needs for energy, to grow, or to heal.

nutritious (new-TRISH-us) Containing nutrients.

protein (PRO-teen) A nutrient that helps your body grow.

recipe (REH-sih-pee) Set of directions for making something to eat.

starch (STARCH) A group of foods that contain carbohydrates.

vitamin C (VY-tah-min SEE) A nutrient that helps your body fight illness and grow strong teeth and healthy gums.

Index